"With rare insight, humour, pathos and irony author Sing Lim has re-created life during the '20s in Vancouver's Chinatown... The style is simple and unadorned and Sing has a delightfully witty perception of his own and other people's foibles and some of the amusing situations in which they find themselves... WEST COAST CHINESE BOY is a sincere and unusual book; it should be purchased for all Canadian libraries..." — *Quill & Quire*

"What sets WEST COAST CHINESE BOY apart from scores of other Chinese American biographies or autobiographies is its refreshing sense of humor and honesty. Here the people are real, with distinct personalities and failings; they aren't stereotypical cardboard characters... Through this small modest book throbs the life of Indians, Chinese, Japanese, East Indians, and Whites. Their stories become our stories. One can ask for little more... get this book and savor it page by page." — *The International Examiner* (Seattle)

"Lim's text and illustrations successfully re-create his family's life... He tells some amazing and terrible things with a very understated delivery."
— *Books in Canada*

"It is an altogether moving and inspiring book — the kind of book one would want children to make their own — with a strong picaresque plot, vividly exotic... Every library must have this book, not simply to adorn a shelf, but to be read, enjoyed and discussed." — *In Review, Canadian Books for Young People*

"Sing Lim not only gives us a child's unique perspective on the quaint and colourful life of Chinatown, but also conveys a sense of living history in his simple yet moving descriptions... Lim's story glows with colour and detail... a rare and fascinating cultural record. It's an opportunity for children to learn, and is certainly a joy to read." — *Kingston Whig Standard*

"It's a delightful book of anecdotes... informative, insightful, honest, and above all, warm and funny."
— *East/West* (San Francisco)

"Sing Lim has carried off both art and anecdote with the sharp report of a Chinese firecracker and the reverberant clash of gongs and cymbals."
— *Canadian Reader*

To the memory of my mother, my sister Nellie and "Uncle" Jing

© 1979, Sing Lim

1991   First paperback edition

Published in Canada by Tundra Books, Montreal, Quebec H3G 1R4 and in the United States by Tundra Books of Northern New York, Plattsburgh, N.Y. 12901.

Library of Congress Card Number: 79-67110

Canadian Cataloging in Publication Data

Lim, Sing, 1915-

   West Coast Chinese Boy

Originally published: Montreal : Tundra, 1979.
ISBN 0-88776-270-0

   1. Lim, Sing, 1915-   2. Chinese Canadians — British Columbia — Vancouver — Biography.   3. Chinese Canadians — British Columbia — Vancouver — Social life and customs.   I. Title.

PS8573.I439W4 1991   971.1'33   C91-090034-5
PR9199.3.L44W4 1991

This edition contains 14 of the color illustrations from the hardcover edition. The original paintings were exhibited at the Art Emporium, Vancouver, in 1980.

The publisher has applied funds from its Canada Council block grant for 1991 toward the editing and production of this book.

Paperback edition design: Dan O'Leary

Printed in Canada by Imprimerie Gagné

West Coast Chinese Boy

SING LIM

Tundra Books

My father

My father's name was Low Lim. He was eighteen years old in 1884 when he came from China to Victoria, B.C. on a sailing ship. The following year the Canadian government required every Chinese to pay a head tax of fifty dollars before he could land. In 1901, the tax rose to $100, and in 1905 to $500. It was a way of keeping Chinese out.

In China, my father worked as a fisherman. In Canada, his first job was cutting down trees in the bush. There he made friends with the Indians; he learned the Chinook jargon – the Indian trade language – and how to survive in the wilderness. He learned a little English too, from the men who collected the cut wood.

My father was one of the first Chinese in Canada to cut his pigtail, or *queue*. That meant he could never return to his native land. Three hundred years before, when the Manchus conquered China, they forced all Chinese to wear pigtails to show they were a vanquished people. Later the Chinese made the *queue* a badge of honor, but reminders of its shameful origin remained – in China, anyone caught without a pigtail (or *sans queue*, as the expression went) was beheaded.

After Father married my mother, he worked as a cobbler, first in Vancouver, then at Steveston and then across the Burrard Inlet near an Indian reservation in North Vancouver. I spent some time with him there when I was six. It was supposed to be punishment for my having put mud pies in our neighbors' mail slots.

Early one morning, my father packed two weeks' supply of groceries and we boarded the ferry. Across the Inlet, the boat banged into the dock several times, shaking all the passengers who were standing, and scaring me. My father reassured me it was all right.

We walked uphill from the terminal to a white building where an Indian boy sat on the steps. He followed us inside. Father took a small parcel from his overcoat and gave it to the boy, talking to him in Chinook. The boy looked at me and ran out. I watched him through the big store window. He limped.

"What's in the parcel?" I asked my father. Who was the Indian boy? Why did he limp? Father said the parcel contained herbal medicine. It was for Mr. Chew, the grocer, who knew about dislocated joints and bones. He was trying to cure the boy.

Next day the boy and I no longer felt like strangers watching each other. He became my friend Johnny. We played games around the water tub used for soaking leather and watched my father mend shoes. He put nails in his mouth, took them out one by one and hammered each in. Finally he got annoyed and ordered us to play in the back room of the shop, which he used as a bedroom and kitchen.

In this room, I first realized the fun of art. We found some worn brushes, two cans of old shoe dyes and a large sheet of crumpled wrapping paper in a garbage can. We nailed down the paper and began to paint. But the dyes only came in two colors, black and brown. We rushed over to

Mr. Chew's store, picked cherries and other fruit out of his garbage can and hurried back. Johnny used a large stone to pound the berries to a pulp. They looked colorful until he added the dyes. Then they looked like something from the outhouse, and even attracted lots of flies. At that point, Father walked in. When he saw the mess, he was furious. For the rest of the day, Johnny and I had to carry in firewood and pile it up beside the stove.

A few days later, at lunch, Johnny and I were in the kitchen with our bowls held out for father to fill with rice. Suddenly an Indian appeared in the doorway. He came so silently and looked so unusual I nearly dropped my bowl. He was tall and lean. A colorful bead design trimmed his hatband, belt, arm bands and leather vest.

Johnny ran to him. The man put down his huge bag and touched Johnny's bad leg. Father said, "Heap skookum," which he later explained to me meant "plenty strong." Then with his chopsticks, he lifted two sow bellies from the large pot. These he carried, one on each chopstick, back to our visitor. They dripped like wet deflated balls.

"Muck-a-muck – eat" Father said. The two men ate. When they finished, the Indian wiped his mouth with the back of his hand and Father wiped his with the inside of his cobbler's apron. Soon they were talking in Chinook, ignoring Johnny and me. I coughed and my father gave us each a meaty soup bone from the pot.

Then from a table drawer, he took out some Chinese straw paper. (This paper had many purposes. It could be used in the outhouse, or as cigarette paper.) Father rolled two cigarettes, fat as cigars. The room filled with smoke as the two men puffed away. Suddenly I understood – this man was Johnny's father.

After they left, Father spread out the contents of the large sack: several deer horns and a newspaper-wrapped bundle. I had never seen my father so happy. Horns were very valuable to the Chinese. He divided the antlers into three piles: "This goes to Mr. Chew for curing Johnny's leg. This will bring a good sum from the herbalist. This one we keep for ourselves."

Then Father opened the bundle wrapped in newspaper. When he saw what was inside, he quickly rewrapped it and said: "We catch the next ferry home."

While he was out of the room, I peeked inside the parcel. What I saw terrified me. It was furry and bloody, and looked like a huge cut-off hand.

Back in Vancouver, our first stop was Uncle Jing's restaurant. When he looked inside the parcel, he, too, was delighted: "It's rare," he said, "to get one so fine and fresh."

What I thought was a hand was really a bear paw!

The bear paw feast

News that Uncle Jing was making preparations for a bear paw feast traveled fast. Everyone wanted to come, so he had to limit the guests to his closest friends. The feast was arranged for the Moon Festival Celebration. This Chinese holiday is like Thanksgiving, but we eat stuffed duck instead of turkey.

When Father and I arrived the morning of the feast, everyone was already busy. Uncle Jing and his brother were making mooncakes and his nephew was plucking ducks. Father was put to work chopping up large blocks of wood into logs small enough to burn. I got the job of sweeping duck feathers off the floor.

Uncle Jing finished the pastries and began to prepare the bear paw. He decided to use the doorless brick oven and leave the regular stove to his assistants. The brick oven was seldom lit, so the cat had made his bed in it. "Get the cat out of there," Uncle Jing ordered me. I put in my hand and pulled its tail, but it only crawled in further. I tugged again and got scratched. This made me mad, so I decided to

try another way. I tossed in a dipperful of cold water. The cat sprang out so fast he knocked over a pot of snails. Uncle Jing yelled when he saw the wet cat flying through the air and the snails all over the floor. He was fond of quoting Confucius, but this time his words were not from any wise man.

It turned out to be a fortunate accident. As I picked the snails up from the floor, Uncle Jing noticed holes had not been tapped in them. He set his brother and me to work with pliers. We had to crack a small opening in each shell to let air in so the guests could draw out the snail meat easily.

Meanwhile, Uncle Jing continued his cooking. Into a steaming pot he put herbs, a whole chicken, a slab of lean pork and cut-up bear paw. He ordered his nephew to add slices of sea slugs and half a bottle of liquor. This was left to cook while Uncle Jing and I set out for the vaudeville show. We returned to find all the guests waiting.

Uncle Jing's party was a great success. His nephew, who wasn't very bright, had poured the whole bottle of liquor into the pot. The guests got tipsy and happy as they ate, particularly the local teacher. My father persuaded him to accept me as a new pupil even though I was under eight, the age for starting Chinese school.

It did not turn out to be such a good arrangement. But at the time, my father – and my mother too when she heard the news – was overjoyed. Like all Chinese parents of Canadian-born children, they wanted us to be proud of being Chinese.

Life in the area

I was born in 1915. We lived on the fifth floor of a huge building on Pender Street. One wing stretched down Shanghai Alley and the other down along the railroad tracks. In the center was a courtyard called Canton Alley.

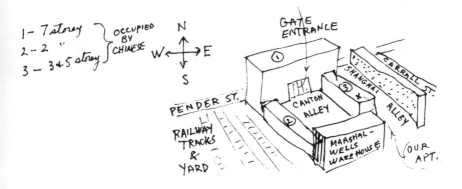

Eight years earlier, rioters had smashed all the windows in the Chinese district and then gone on to attack the Japanese. The new building was meant to protect us in case of future riots. It had only one entrance with an iron gate that could be closed in an emergency, like a prison or a fort. On the ground floor were thirteen shops.

We had a small parlor, two bedrooms, a kitchen and a washroom. The only heat came from a small stove in the parlor and the cookstove in the kitchen. Fuel was expensive and precious. As children we picked up spilled coal along the railroad tracks near the building, and our neighbors searched the streets for discarded wood crates.

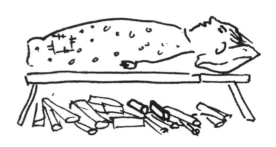

We were the only family there with our own hot-water system. A friend of my father's built it. In winter an open barrel of water stood near the kitchen stove. A pipe carried the cold water to a flat coil of pipes inside the firebox of the stove where it was heated; another pipe took the hot water back to the barrel. It worked, though I never knew why.

Families bought wood by the wagonload. It was dumped in the street for the wood carriers to haul into the houses or up the narrow stairs of apartment buildings. There was no storage space, so some kept the wood under their beds to dry out. The beds were narrow planks propped on two sawhorses.

We used every inch of space, even the fire escapes outside. There we hung fish (usually flounder) and mustard greens to dry.

13

The apartment below

About twenty single men lived in the apartment below us. They were seldom all there at once because many did shift work or were out of town doing seasonal work; that way they could take turns using the beds.

They also took turns using the stove to cook, and while they waited they smoked water pipes and talked. Their kitchen was warm and friendly. I liked to sit quietly and listen to them tell of China and how they were conscripted to come to Canada. From them I learned of the great fire of 1886 that destroyed much of the Chinese area of Vancouver, and of the racial riots of 1907.

They talked too of the thousands of coolies from Northern China who were kept locked up in boxcars on the railroad tracks alongside our building. They were being taken across Canada and sent on to France to dig trenches during World War I. (In 1916-17, more than 200,000 passed through Canada this way.) People from our building would go down, talk to the frightened men and pass food into the cars.

It was in the apartment downstairs that I saw Western art for the first time. I was six years old, and I still remember the colored pictures that covered the walls of the small parlor, and the black and white prints that lined the hallways. One picture I especially loved. It was a snow scene with hunters on a hilltop followed by a pack of hounds and birds flying overhead. (I would later discover it was a reproduction of a famous painting, *Winter Scene*, by the Flemish master, Pieter Breughel.) Mr. Sam, one of

the men who lived in the apartment, had worked as a
janitor for more than fifty years in offices, stores and
theaters. When pictures were thrown out, he salvaged
them to brighten up the place.

The drug store

Of all the shops on the ground floor of our building, my
favorites were the drug store and the poultry shop.

Mr. Kwong, the druggist, was really an herbalist. His
remedies were mostly vegetable, though a few – as we
shall see – were animal. I ran errands for him, so I knew
his shop well.

He had a queer contraption with suspended leather
handles that looked like a unicycle. It had a heavy metal
wheel that rocked back and forth inside the groove of a
big mortar. Mr. Kwong would stand on the shaft of the
wheel and grind away, turning roots into powder.

Hundreds of little drawers contained herbs: ginseng, seeds, dried buds and blossoms, taro roots, bark and seaweed. Other drawers held stranger things: dried insects, rhino skins, dried snakes and lizards and animal horns. Mr. Kwong used a crude-looking scale to weigh each ingredient. He said it measured accurately and because leaves were very light, exact amounts were important.

He often brewed herbal teas; a mixture of herbs in three or four cups of water boiled down to one cup. Most of them had a bitter unpleasant taste, so Mr. Kwong always included a small package of raisins or a few black dates to help the patients swallow the tea. One of his concoctions was surprisingly popular: alcohol mixed with snake venom. He made it by soaking live rattlesnakes in alcohol.

The fresher the venom, the more powerful the potion. Mr. Kwong prescribed it for people with rheumatism. Mr. Kwong used a lot of alcohol in his medicines. Sometimes he sent my brother York, a teamster, to bring it from the illegal stills run by farmers on Lulu Island. My brother let me go with him. It was a long slow trip. To keep me from falling off the wagon, he fastened me to the driver's seat with a rope.

The poultry shop

If Mr. Kwong's drug store was the most mysterious place on our block, the most colorful and lively was Mr. Sak's poultry shop. What sights and sounds!

Chickens in wooden cages, pigeons in small wire cages and ducks in big round rattan containers cackled, cooed and quacked on the street outside the store and up front just inside.

The chickens came in different sizes and breeds to suit the varied customers. The Chinese would not buy White Leghorns, if they could get Plymouth Rock hens. East Indians liked large old roosters. One particular East Indian sect even had Mr. Sak chop up the roosters into small pieces.

At the back of the shop a special place with tagged live chickens was set aside for the Hebrew rabbi. Most of Mr. Sak's customers gave their orders early in the day and picked up the cleaned birds later, but his Jewish clients had to wait until the rabbi next came to perform the kosher preparations.

Unfortunately for Mr. Sak, his shop was lively in another way. We children loved to play there; we made Indian headdresses, darts and arrows with the feathers. It was the way we got the feathers that caused trouble. When Mr. Sak was busy at the back of the store, we grabbed a fowl and pulled out its tail feathers. Its screeches brought Mr. Sak screaming after us. But we weren't always up to mischief. When a chicken escaped, we captured it for Mr. Sak. He appreciated us then.

School and school

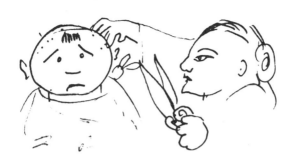

My mother sat me down and cut off all my hair, leaving only a small comb-like patch on my forehead. The arranged-for day had come. That night I would start Chinese school. I was already going to regular public school in the daytime and liked it. But Chinese school was another matter. I looked like a jailbird, and felt like one too. I would now spend every evening, Monday to Friday from seven to nine, in class.

My teacher was at his desk reading as I entered the classroom. He looked at me and went back to reading without a word. Hours seemed to pass. Finally he waved his bamboo cane at me and pointed to an empty desk.

I sat down with my brush, my ink jar and copybook. Everyone around me was busy writing. I tried to look busy too, but soon got bored. I took out a little box of grasshoppers I captured earlier that day and turned them loose. Soon they were hopping about the classroom and everybody was laughing – except the teacher. He smacked me over the head with his bamboo cane.

For a few evenings after that, fear of his cane kept me busy at my lessons. Then a new idea occurred. Every evening before I left home, I padded my legs and arms with magazines under my long stockings and sleeves. Most important, under my cap, I stuffed a folded newspaper. Now that I was protected, I found a new escape from dull lessons. I drew pictures with my brush instead of practicing Chinese writing. I loved drawing and decided that one day I would be an artist.

Even in public school I spent a lot of time drawing. I was lucky to be put in a mixed class with white children instead of in one of the classes with only Chinese. My father told me that earlier all the Chinese pupils in Victoria were taken out of the public schools and put in a segregated school. (Chinese parents refused to send their children to school for a whole year until this was changed.)

My school – Central Public – had a reputation of fairness toward the Chinese. The teachers did not discriminate

between pupils of different backgrounds. This was rare then when our people were called "the yellow peril."

In third grade I had a wonderful teacher called Miss Scott who encouraged me in my drawing. A new art school had opened in the attic of our school building and she took one of my drawings to show the director. It was a proud moment for me.

Sometimes I wished my teachers could be with me outside the classroom too, because we had trouble with the white kids on our way to and from school. We walked in groups for protection, the small kids following closely behind the bigger, stronger boys. Our parents forbade us to fight but we often disobeyed them, even though they punished us if they found out. We just couldn't walk away from catcalls like, "Hey, yellow bellies," or "Cowards."

I once came home with a black eye, and my mother was very upset. I told her I had won the fight, but it didn't make her any happier.

RECITE FROM MEMORY.

Being Chinese

I was not allowed to speak English at home or with other children. Our parents suffered so much racial intolerance they did not want to be part of Canadian culture. The older Chinese looked down on us who were born in Canada. They called us "siwash" and "half-bread" (half-breed). The word "siwash" was what some whites called the Indians. It meant "a red savage." possibly coming from the French word "sauvage." When an older Chinese used it, he meant "native, without Chinese culture." It was not a nice name to be called, whatever its exact meaning.

Chinese school was important because there I would – my parents hoped – learn about our culture and how to write Chinese with a brush. There were sixty students in my class. The classroom was in the old meeting hall of the Chinese Empire Reform Association built in 1903 to encourage students from China to study Western thought and science. The society no longer existed, but one photograph on the wall showed Chinese men dressed in suits and stiff round-cornered collars, posing in front of chemistry lab equipment: a Bunsen burner, thistle tube, flask and test tube. Another photo showed a crowd standing around a model steam engine.

Learning to write Chinese

The Chinese write with a brush. This style of writing is called calligraphy. It is an ancient handwriting invented by Ts'ang-Chieh who lived in the 25th century B.C. He watched the patterns made by ants crawling on the ground and birds flying in the air, then copied them down. The pictures he made formed the basis of Chinese written words, or characters.

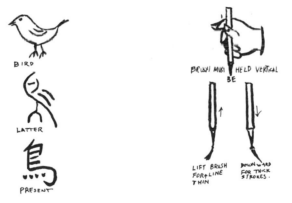

In early Chinese writing, the character for a bird looked very much like a bird. But the language changed and developed over the years. Today it would be difficult for someone who has not learned Chinese to guess the picture within the character. I have shown how the word for "bird" changed.

Our teacher taught us to hold the brush straight up, like a pole. To get a thick line you press down on the tip of the brush. Thin lines need less pressure. To keep us from gripping the brush too tightly, he put a wad of paper in our palms. He showed us how to pick up ink from the ink jar. If we put too much on the tip of the brush, it spread all over the absorbent straw or rice paper. The jar was filled with "hog's belly cotton" to soak up the excess ink: this is a cotton-like material without lint.

We learned to write by tracing over Chinese characters.

THE INK PAD

GRINDING OUR OWN INK.

My mother

My mother's name was Chow Shee. In Hong Kong her family had been in the textile business, but most of them died in a cholera epidemic. Only she and a brother survived. Mother told us how rats entered houses, ran around in circles and dropped dead. Shortly after, the people who lived in the houses died too. Their bodies were wrapped in straw mats and tossed into the water.

My father learned about her through friends who advised him to send for her. She arrived in Vancouver to marry Father just before 1900. She was fifteen. I had four older brothers and a sister, Nellie. She was four years older than I, and a great help to Mother. She cleaned the house, shopped and picked up clothing from the local tailor shops for Mother to alter or mend. Mother used her Singer sewing machine when she could, but did most of the work by hand. Sewing machines couldn't make buttonholes sixty years ago. Then buttons were used everywhere zippers and belts are now. A pair of trousers had six buttons for the suspenders alone.

The extra income helped feed the family. When there was any money left over, Mother gave it to Nellie to spend on special foods like oyster crackers, oatmeal, Cream of Wheat, canned soups, and meat for making Western meals. She often brought me a treat of doughnuts or animal crackers inside cartons shaped like a circus wagon. Everything might cost less than a dollar, but it made us very very happy. Sometimes Mother prepared liver and onions. This was a special meal for us because we got to eat it in a new way – with a knife and fork instead of chopsticks.

Mother was a gentle, kind person who was always helping the neighbors. She died when I was fourteen years old.

Kind and cruel guardians

Kee was a little boy suffering from a bone disease called rickets. He was sent to this country for a cure. He lived with his uncle who was part owner of a tailor shop. Kee and I met there and became friends right away. I often

visited the shop – sometimes to pick up cloth or thread for Mother, sometimes just to play with the empty spools lying about.

It was a happy day for Kee's uncles when my little friend returned home from the hospital. The doctor told him he might be able to straighten Kee's legs with braces. But Kee hated them and was very depressed. When the other kids saw his metal braces they nicknamed him "Crippled Kee." This hardly improved Kee's mood, and he kept to himself most of the time.

One day his uncle decided to do something to lift Kee's spirits. He built a huge kite, one with special features. It looked like a strange insect with two antennae and a round disc attached to each "wing." The bright, intense colors made it look almost grotesque!

Our first day out was very exciting. Kee's uncle started the kite off low in the sky, then handed us the string. But it looked so big and scary neither of us wanted to handle it. So Kee's uncle had to fly the kite himself. While it soared higher and higher, the whistling sound made by the two discs grew louder. We were so spellbound, none of us noticed the policeman. He made us stop. The kite was frightening all the horses. Some had bolted and were running down the street, dragging wagons without drivers! That ended the kite flying, but Kee thought it had been great fun.

Some children were mistreated. I remember one mean, miserable old man who lived near us. Everybody in the neighborhood disliked him because of the way he treated a small boy who was sent to this country and placed under his guardianship.

One winter he locked the boy outside in the cold for hours without a coat. The neighbors felt sorry for the boy, but

did not want to interfere. They felt parents and guardians had the right to bring up a child any way they chose.

He even sent the boy to school barefoot. The teachers thought he wore no shoes because he was poor, so they bought him a pair. But soon afterward he appeared at school barefoot again.

Finally, the school sent the truant officer to his home to investigate. My brother went along as interpreter. His threat to call the police put a stop, for a while anyway, to the old man's cruel treatment.

Baby's head shave

When a baby was about to be born, Mother and some other women volunteers went to the expectant woman's home. They prepared ginger root, pig's feet, eggs, cane sugar and black fungus, placed it all in two huge pots of vinegar and boiled the mixture for several hours. After the baby arrived, the mother did not have to cook. She could use the food as a steady diet for a couple of weeks. It was

nourishing and, according to Mother, "a blood purifier."
Even today this food is served to well-wishers who come
to see a new baby. In return, they bring the baby "lucky
money" wrapped in Chinese red paper.

When the baby was a month old, my mother prepared for
another celebration called "baby's head shave." This time
Mother made pastries at home for the party. Nellie boiled
the special red paper for wrapping "lucky money" to get a
liquid dye. Eggs were placed in the dye and cooked until
hard boiled. Mother and Nellie made huge quantities of
red eggs for the baby's mother to give to the guests at the
party.

Over at the baby's house other women prepared for the
big dinner. Along with the usual banquet goodies,
"chicken wine" soup was served. This is a traditional
Chinese soup made with chicken, ginger, black fungus
and wine. (Friends who were unable to come got eggs
delivered in a bag with a slice of barbecued pork or boiled
chicken. More "lucky money" was given in return.)
Everybody enjoyed the party – except maybe the baby
who had its hair shaved off. On the partially bald head,
the women placed a funny-looking ceremonial bonnet
with jade and gold ornaments pinned around it. To me it
looked like a Mickey Mouse cap. According to Chinese
custom, the one-month-old baby was already one year old.

The man I worked for

When I was nine years old, my father sent me to work for the summer on a farm. Mr. Lam was once a peddler of buns and coffee, and was teased in the Chinese gambling houses around Vancouver because he was a Christian. Now he owned a general store, a pickle factory and one of the biggest farms on Lulu Island in the Fraser River. My father had loaned him fifty dollars to start his farm, and Mr. Lam returned the favor by giving me a job. I was probably more nuisance to him than real help that first summer, but that didn't make me like him any more. He was just too strict.

I returned to the farm every summer during my school years, but I remember the first summer best. I have tried to describe it in imaginary letters to my mother.

The summer heat was awful. Our bunkhouse was an oven. We worked from 6:30 in the morning to 7:30 at night every day except Sunday when we finished at noon. But funny things happened to cheer us up.

One day Mr. Lam got a great idea. He thought of a way to enrich a field and produce a prize crop of broccoli. He went to the local fish cannery and asked for their waste: spoiled salmon, fish heads, innards. The plant manager was delighted. It saved him dumping the garbage into the river. We moved wagons and wagons of the putrid stuff out into the fields. Mr. Lam watched us, very pleased with himself. Afterward it took us hours to wash the smell of rotten fish off our bodies.

But Mr. Lam was not so happy as he looked out over the field the next morning. Everywhere cats and dogs were crazily digging up the fish remains and chasing each other around. Mr. Lam ordered us to rebury what was left in deeper soil. We were all laughing so hard we didn't mind – or almost didn't mind.

Dear Mom,   July 22, 1923

I eat breakfast at 5:30 and start work at 6:30 oclock. I can't sleep because people make noise when they sleep. One even sings in his sleep. I work all day pulling weeds with a nice old man, Mr. Wong – too tired to walk home at 7:30 at nite.

Your son, Sing

ohnny and I watched my father
mend shoes.

A strange-looking visitor suddenly
appeared.

Uncle Jing's party was a huge success. Into a steaming pot he put herbs,
a whole chicken, a slab of lean pork and cut-up bear paw.

While they waited to use the cookstove, they smoked water pipes.

The drawers held dried insects, snakes and lizards, rhino skins and animal horns.

East Indians liked large old roosters.

My parents hoped I would learn Chinese culture.

Nellie shopped and Mother sewed.

The women put a funny bonnet on baby's bald head.

The werewolf turned into a beautiful woman, but not completely.

The Buddhist monk fought off evil demons (scene from "The Monkey King").

I hung around Uncle Jing's restaurant and he kept an eye on me.

After we returned from the cemetery, we cut the roasted pig into strips.

We built a Chinese snowman to celebrate the New Year. It rains most of the winter in Vancouver, but one year everything was white.

Dear Mom,

Mr. Lam is not a bad man. He lets me work in his pickle factory when it's raining outside. Japanese women and girls my age work there too. They pick out big and small sizes and put them in barrels. My job is to take away the big and old ones with a cart. They are polite people and nice. Mr Wong taught me to say good morning and thank you to them *o-hi-o* and *ah-le-ga-tor*. I like to talk Japanese because it is not hard to know. I don't think Mr. Wong knows much because often he talks Chinook to them. He gets mad when they talk too much. He says *hy-iu- wau wau* and *halo skookum* when they want him to lift heavy things. That means "enough talk" and "not strong."

Yesterday Mr. Lam asked me to go to church with him and his family. I stayed at the farm instead and did not miss the chicken supper. When he brings me home and gives my money to you, Mom, can I have some for seeing some Buck Jones and Tom Mix cowboy movies?

Love, Sing

Dear Mom,

Today I pulled up onions and let them dry by the sun. For shipping to a place named Australia. I work by myself, far away sometimes and have no watch. I put a stick in the ground like I saw in a picture at School called sundial. I took the alarm clock you gave me and was not late for lunch again. We eat lunch outside the house. Inside was too hot. Bugs and leafs fall on the rice. I am too hungry to worry.

Sing

your clock

Dear Mom,

Today is Sunday. We don't have to work in the afternoon and we wash our dirty clothes. Mr. Wong cooks some corn in the patch for us to eat. Also he gives some to the Japanese ladies and girls. They laugh all the time and joke and make my face red. There are more than 40 of them working for Mr. Lam. I like them but keep away because I feel uncomfortable.

this is corn cooked by us

I like today the most because Mr. Lam stayed away all day at church and we had chicken again for dinner. I wish every day was Sunday. Other days Mr. Lam spies on us with his field glass and we have to work hard.

Sometimes I like to watch the night sky and sometimes I get sick all over. When can I come home, Mom?

Sing

Dear Mom,

Mr. Wong took me to see a lady named Bing Bing Cum San to tell her to work at our tomato glass house tomorrow. She teaches little girls dancing and how to wave small fans on Sundays. She makes music with something like a box, only there's lots of strings on top. I didn't go inside her house because I didn't want to take my shoes off. Mr. Wong says it is polite to keep my shoes outside before going into any Japanese house. They are built close together and on water, only they are raised up with large poles.

Afterward, he took me to the cannery to get some fish heads. There are lots of Chinese working in the cannery. Some of them get 20 cents an hour and some are contract workers. They do all kinds of work.

We didn't stay long here and watch because our cook needed the fish heads for supper.

Your son, Sing

cutting Fish

Sealing cans by hand

Boiling hot Water And LYe

washing Packed Cans

Of werewolves and Chinese opera

At one baby's head shave party, I noticed a woman who could not move around without help. When we got home, I asked Mother what was the matter with her. She explained that the woman could not walk because her feet were bound back in China when she was a little girl. I was very curious; the Chinese in Canada never followed this custom and I wanted to know more about it.

Mother told me a story of how it all started.

A werewolf once transformed itself into a beautiful woman. The emperor fell in love with her and made her his empress. But the courtiers around the palace noticed something strange about her. She had very tiny feet which she tried to hide under her long robe.

She had not been able to change completely from werewolf to woman. Her hind paws remained small, much smaller than human feet.

She realized she was in danger if the truth about her origins got out, so she thought up a clever plan. She suggested to the emperor the smaller a woman's feet were, the more beautiful she was. The emperor accepted the new standard of beauty. Soon the ladies of the court started to bind their daughters' feet to keep them small, and the custom spread.

My mother took me to parties and Uncle Jing took me to the opera. Going to the opera was like going to the movies today. Then the older people didn't have much to do in the evening, so the opera was a wonderful escape.

It took place every evening and lasted four hours. Sometimes three or four people used the same ticket, taking turns to watch the play. Uncle Jing went nearly every night but, because I was so young, my parents let me go only on special occasions.

Most of the plays were in the Mandarin language of Northern China. My people were from Southern China and spoke Cantonese, so often we did not understand what the actors were saying.

A RIDE IN A CHARIOT.

THE NIGHT WITH "UNCLE" JING
AT THE OPERA

The opera

The theater was nearby on Columbia Street. Sometimes it got so noisy we could hear it from our apartment. Children ran about, mothers nursed their babies and everyone munched on snacks. Orange peels and peanut shells littered the floor. The orchestra sat on one side of the stage. There was no scenery except for a table and some chairs. But the costumes were magnificent.

Usually the plays were adapted from classical Chinese novels. They ranged from tear jerkers – very popular with the adults – to my favorite, the martial type with battle scenes. I remember one play called "The Monkey King" about a real person from the seventh century called Tripitaka. According to legend he made a dangerous journey from China to India escorted by his disciples – a monkey, a pig and a monk – to bring back Buddhist scriptures. Along the way many gods came to his aid to fight off evil demons.

The most beautiful concubine

The opera I remember best was not part of the classical Chinese theater, and I remember it for reasons other than its artistic merit.

It was a play about the most beautiful concubine in China. The theater advertised a bathing scene where the actress would appear in "the most revealing swimsuit."

When we arrived at the theater, it was already packed. Fortunately, Uncle Jing had reserved seats in the front row to give himself ample room to smoke his water pipe.

The first part of the play was boring. People coughed because of the cold and the smoke. Then the bright stage lights dimmed. It was the moment we were waiting for – the bathing scene! Two actresses appeared on stage. One played the maiden attendant and held a towel to hide the body of the lead actress. As they moved slowly toward the center of the stage, the lights grew dimmer. Finally, the stage was so dark only their silhouettes were visible. Then came the climax. The maiden attendant moved aside and made her exit, leaving the beautiful star standing alone. In the dim light, she looked completely nude.

Suddenly the bright stage lights were switched on. What we saw was not a naked woman at all! She was wearing tightly fitted Stanfield underwear. The poor actress was so confused and embarrassed she ran off the stage like a scared rabbit. The audience roared with laughter.

Uncle Jing found out afterward what had happened. The stagehand was supposed to turn the lights out completely to allow the actress in long johns to make a quick exit in the dark, but had pulled the wrong switch, he said, "by mistake."

The viaduct people

Uncle Jing was not my real uncle. We just called him that because he was so good to everyone. My father was often away from home, working or drinking with friends, and from the time I was very small I hung around Uncle Jing's restaurant. I was often up to mischief, so my mother liked Uncle Jing to keep an eye on me. I was lucky to have such a kind guardian.

We called them "the viaduct people" because they lived under the Georgia viaduct about three blocks from our street. They built themselves shelters – with corrugated iron and wood from discarded crates – just large enough to crawl into for sleeping. Sometimes a wooden crate was simply covered over with dirt and looked like a cave. Ten men might live there. They were not rubby dubs or winos. They were men who had been rejected by society and given up hope. They seldom gave us trouble, and we gave them none. They only came into our area to get water from stores when their supply of rainwater ran out, or to search for food in garbage cans.

They were of all nationalities. Among them was a Chinese man I remember well. It was a "lousy" experience. One day I returned home from Uncle Jing's restaurant, scratching my head. My mother examined my hair for fleas and was horrified to find I had lice. She undressed and bathed me, then cut off all my hair and rubbed my bald head with kerosene. Later that evening Father came home and said itchy customers were complaining that Uncle Jing was running "a lousy joint." It turned out that Uncle Jing, with his usual generosity, was letting the Chinese derelict eat scraps off the table in his restaurant. From that day on, Uncle Jing fed him outside in the back alley.

Tongs

Tongs were family or clan organizations. We belonged to the Lim tong (sometimes spelled Lam or Lum), one of the largest in Canada. The tong helped members with money problems and protected them from outsiders. At the meetings, complaints were heard against any member who had not acted rightly.

There were many tongs or family associations in Vancouver's Chinese community. One of the most colorful was the Gee Gung Tong, or the Chinese Free Masons. It started as a secret society and haven for nationalists who hoped to free China from the rule of the Manchu dynasty. They called themselves Free Masons because it made them sound like a legitimate secret society to Westerners, although they were not recognized by the true Free Masons. After the Manchu dynasty fell in 1911, it stopped being secretive and members wore the Chinese Free Mason insignia buttons on their lapels. Even today, this society is very active in local Chinese affairs.

I had two good reasons for attending our tong's meetings – Uncle Jing's sharp tongue and his delicious hot black bean buns. He would bake a large amount and serve them after the meeting. I could hardly wait to eat, but first I had to work. Uncle Jing ordered me to bring chairs to the front hall from the storage space at the back of the kitchen, place spittoons in convenient spots, put teacups on the committee table and clean the chairs with a long duster.

A DAY WITH "UNCLE" JING.

Sometimes, when Uncle Jing wasn't looking, I dusted off the tong's cat too. Just before the end of the meeting, I was sent to pick up the oven-fresh buns at Uncle Jing's restaurant a couple of stores away.

Sometimes I had to go alone to the Chinese Free Mason tong to look for one of my brothers who was a member. It was a scary place. To get to the social room where he hung out, I had to cross the meeting hall. It was a huge room, silent and empty, with a temple-like arrangement at the far end. A life-size wooden idol of Kwan Kung, the god of war worshipped by the members, stood among smaller ones of the warrior's three brothers. The grotesque carvings were surrounded by heavy draperies and painted in vivid red, green and gold. The colors and odd shapes under the temple lights were very spooky. The smell of burning joss sticks made it even more eerie.

I would run across the room as fast as I could, remembering the horror story of a spy who tried to infiltrate a secret tong meeting. He was discovered and hacked up into small pieces by the members. Each had to eat a piece to share the guilt in case the law, or the spirit of the dead man, returned to punish them.

No wonder I ran fast.

Offerings to the dead

One of my favorite festivals was Ch'ing Ming, our annual remembrance day, when offerings to the dead were made. It took place around Easter. Uncle Jing was in charge of preparing everything and taking it to the Mountain View Cemetery in South Vancouver. Into a hired truck we loaded barbecued pig, boiled chicken, hard-boiled eggs, bowls of rice, fruit, pastries, cigarettes, beer and wine. I carried a huge paper bag filled with joss sticks, "money" and "clothes." There were sheets of straw paper with a silver symbol in the center.

At the burial grounds, four men carried the heavy wooden tray containing the roasted pig to the altar – a large cement table built years before with Chinese contributions. The rest of the food was put next to the pig. On the far side of the altar we placed burning joss sticks. Two men made a fire in the oven beside the altar and burned the paper "money" and "clothes." We then took the burning joss sticks and walked up and down the burial ground looking for our tong members' graves. On each we put two joss sticks.

We finally reloaded the food on the truck. By that time, a truck from another tong would have arrived, waiting to use the altar.

When we returned to the meeting hall, we found the back kitchen floor well scrubbed and newspaper spread out in the center. The greasy wooden tray was placed there and the roasted pig was cut into strips. The strips were put in packages, marked with the name of the donor and the amount of money contributed.

After we feasted on the food brought back from the cemetery, we delivered the little packages to everyone who had supported the outing. By the end of the day we were exhausted but happy. I liked to think of our dead relatives having "a big meal," "money" to spend and new "clothing" to wear.

Christmas and Chinese New Year

To the average Chinese family like ours, Christmas was just another day. Mr. Lam, still grateful to my father, sent a bottle of liquor. That was the only thing that happened.

But to the Chinese peddlers, it was an important time. Many Chinese peddled fish and vegetables to earn a living. Their routes went all over Vancouver, spanning as much as five miles. The peddlers were polite, dependable and honest, and well liked by the white community. Just before Christmas they wrapped little packages of candied ginger, lai-chee nuts or tea to give to friends and customers. Many of them were in areas without stores or regular transportation and, for some, their Chinese peddler was the only person to visit at Christmas with a little gift. To this day, many white people of my generation remember those visits with pleasure.

Although we didn't celebrate Christmas, we children were not too disappointed because the Chinese Lunar New Year followed only a month or so later. Our mother dressed us up and gave us haircuts. We were given "lucky

money" (*lai see*) to buy candy and firecrackers. We visited homes, stores and tong community centers where we could help ourselves to dried candied sweets, water chestnuts, coconuts, lotus and red watermelon seeds. They were set out in wooden boxes with eight containers, all beautifully lacquered. Near the boxes were fruit, pastries and a pot of tea in a rattan basket lined with cloth to keep it warm.

Back at the apartment, Mother was busy preparing the chicken given us by Mr. Jake. He had a small pig and chicken farm outside town, and a few days before New Year's he gave us and other families a live chicken. Mr. Jake appreciated our having saved scraps of food throughout the year to use as slop for his pigs.

It was a happy occasion when it snowed around our New Year's, just as it is around Christmas time. It rains most of the winter in Vancouver, but I remember one year when everything was white. The color of our holiday seemed all the brighter. On the way home from school we built a real Chinese snowman with a colorful bib. The younger children flew their balloons, while one boy set off firecrackers.

Times to remember

Festivals occurred only once a year, but two events I much enjoyed could happen any time, and I was always ready.

One was the sound of music coming from the apartment below ours. It was a signal for me to rush down to watch and listen. The movements of the music makers and the shape of their instruments fascinated me. One guitar looked like a large frying pan. Another was shaped like a wooden mallet with pear-shaped wedges at the end of a long handle. The banjo had a sound box covered in snakeskin. The strings on the instruments were made of "catgut," not wire, so it was not surprising that the sounds they made seemed as if they really came from some animal.

The "conductor" tapped on a hardwood block with two small drumsticks. The "tok tok" of his drum kept the other musicians in rhythm. But sometimes he and the cymbal player made too much noise and the neighbors yelled.

The sounds were all terrible, and I loved them. Most of all I liked listening to the flute – but only in the apartment and during the daytime. To hear a flute at night frightened me. Any child would be scared if he grew up among people as superstitious as we were. We believed the melancholy notes of the flute attracted ghosts.

Funerals

The other event that could happen any time – but never happened often enough for me – was the funeral of a rich man. It was always the best parade in town.

Because there was so much anti-Chinese prejudice in Vancouver in those days, we often tried to westernize our looks and behavior so we would not attract attention. Our newspapers and community leaders told us to wear Western clothing and shoes instead of Chinese garb and slippers.

A rich Chinese man's funeral, however, seemed planned to attract attention. It was an attempt to "gain face" or prestige. People lined the street to watch. A Western band, hired from one of the rowdy vaudeville theaters, dressed up in neat uniforms and led the march, playing the famous funeral dirge. (I think they were more at ease in their burlesque theater.) An open car followed, carrying a huge blown-up portrait of the deceased. Then came more cars piled up with flowers and wreaths, then the family car, then the hearse. Behind that walked a group of mourners – the honored guests and tong representatives. To me they didn't look at all mournful in their top hats, tuxedos, winged-collar shirts, white gloves and spats. They looked like performers from the minstrel show.

These were followed by folk dressed in common clothing such as bib overalls. Behind them, a long line of cars – the richer the dead man, the more cars.

Finally, Mac's Moving Van brought up the rear. Mac was a white Canadian who often hired out his truck for such occasions. On it rode the Chinese orchestra from the opera house. The music from their cymbals, horns, drums and gong was punctuated with the loud backfire of Mac's truck.

We kids, me among them, ran along after it. The parade ended at the edge of the Chinese district, and the mourners were driven to the cemetery.

What a way to say goodbye!

Afterword – the years since

I have tried to unlock my memory.

Nearly all of the people I have described have long since gone to join their noble ancestors. One who is still alive is my Chinese school teacher, Lim Hon Yuen. We have long ago forgiven each other for those old school days. I visited him a few months ago at his son's home where he now lives – he's in his eighties – and we talked and laughed together over those old days.

Because life was so difficult for the Chinese in Vancouver, the kindness of many people shines brightly for me across the years. The gentle nature of my mother is my first memory, and of my sister, Nellie, but most of all there is Uncle Jing, absolutely the most lovable and generous person I have ever known.

Those crazy nights I spent with him at the opera played an important part in my life as an artist. Fifteen years later, I returned (with my fellow student Bill Kinnis now of *The Gazette* in Montreal), drawn back by the memory of how the players moved on the stage. Uncle Jing had died. I was attending art classes during the day, and for two years I went every night to the opera house to make quick action and gesture sketches as part of my art training.

The name Scott stands out because of two people, unrelated except in my memory. It was the name of my third grade teacher – I remember her only as "Miss" Scott – at Central School who encouraged me in my art; it was also the name of the head of the art school she showed my drawing to. Twelve years later I met him for the first time, and studied art under him – Charles H. Scott, one of the founders and principal of the Vancouver Art School.

A very happy time was the two-year period from 1945 to 1947 I spent at the National Film Board in Ottawa. So many people helped and encouraged me: Joel Barg, Al Barkes, Donald Buchanan, Carl Dair, Alma Duncan, Guy Glover, Bill Kinnis, Joe Licastro, Jack Long, Ian Lindsay, Norman McLaren, Mrs. Dorothy McPherson, P.K. Page, John Ritchie.

Another important influence in my life then was artist Henri Masson. He was a genuine friend who let me use his studio, took me on sketching trips and introduced me to the difficult technique of doing monotypes, a medium I still like. All of the paintings in this book are monotypes: I paint on glass, then blot paper down on top to make a print. Only one painting results, and it must be right or it is thrown away. Like a spontaneous drawing, it cannot be corrected.

I returned to Vancouver in the late '40s, and then to Steveston and the farm where I had worked as a boy. There I found the quiet I needed to paint. But it was a heartbreaking experience. All of my Japanese friends were gone. Two terrible events had changed their lives since the days we worked together. When Japan invaded China in the 1930s, many Chinese in Vancouver boycotted everything Japanese, and the farm where I had worked refused to hire Japanese. Then came World War II, when everyone of Japanese origin on the West Coast was sent inland to internment camps. Everywhere I went on sketching trips in the area I found vacant homes and abandoned shacks.

But the months spent there were fruitful. I produced many drawings and paintings and on a return trip to Ottawa, I showed them to Mr. Donald Buchanan, art critic, a former editor of *Canadian Art* magazine and director at the National Gallery. Through his recommendation, I was offered a one-man show by Agnes Lefort at her Montreal gallery. Miss Lefort, a great lady, opened the first art gallery in Canada devoted exclusively to modern art.

The struggle between being Chinese and being Canadian, between Chinese culture that was so important to my parents' generation and Canadian culture, I resolved in my own way. I found in art a more universal culture, and I wish I had done more with it. I went to work for various printers in Vancouver, and for the past twenty years I owned and operated my own small print shop there. It enabled me to marry and support children, but it also meant I had little time or energy to spare. I sold my shop last year. The paintings and drawings in this book represent my return to art after a long absence. My thanks to Mrs. May Cutler and Jane Moore of Tundra Books whose encouragement and help made this return possible.

As I look back on the events of my childhood, some of which happened over sixty years ago, I feel many emotions: love and gratitude, amazement and fear, anger and frustration, but most of all, the urge to laugh. Recently, someone who knew a little of the terrible treatment suffered by Chinese Canadians through the

years asked me: "How did you survive it?" "By laughing,"
I said. "It is the sense of humor of the Chinese that helps
us live through the unlivable."

Today, across the decades, that laughter still sounds in my
ears. As I look at my three daughters I realize how little
they know of what their parents and grandparents went
through, how few their hardships are by comparison. But
they don't laugh as much either. They haven't as much to
laugh about.

Sing Lim

Vancouver, B.C., 1979